every *bit of the girl*

EVERY BIT OF THE GIRL

poems inspired by women of history

CAY BLUESTOCKING

PENFOLD

Penfold Publishing

Front cover by Candice MacAllister

Published by Penfold Publishing

Printed in the United Kingdom
First Printing: October 2024

25 24 23 22 21 20 19 18   10 9 8 7 6 5 4 3 2 1

ISBN 978-1-8360-2994-6

To my nieces, H. R. and N.

I never knew what it was to cry tears of joy before you.

CONTENTS

Womanhood is a network of all the women
that shape the woman we become.

From our mothers to those who mother us.

The girls we go through girlhood with
and those who grew with us into womanhood.

Women never die alone because our network,
grows as we grow.

Kangwa Nora Musonda

FOREWORD

While the poetry of this book is greatly inspired by significant women throughout world history, these poems are not meant to act as primary or secondary sources for their stories. As usual, art and media portrayals will only offer glimpses into the lives of people of the past and the work of both public and academic historians ought not to be overlooked. The nature of a select few women in the collection—Eve, Lilith, Khadija, Jael and Mahapajapati Gotami—is more of a theological, and some would say mythological, nature and will not have the same date range as other women in the collection, but from the tales and records of them have birthed many concepts and ideas of womanhood and thus act as further precursors to the collection.

The omission of anyone in particular from this poetry collection does not mean that they are any less valuable or significant to history, just as the omission of so many women from history does not mean that their roles were never played. The lengths or styles of each poem vary and the length or style of a particular poem does not denote more or less value as a person or as a subject of study. If there is a woman from history who resonates with you and inspires you, whether that is a woman included in this collection or not, I encourage you to let that inspiration lead you to creation.

It is also worth noting that the goal of this collection is to make space for all women to be heard. I have made as much of an effort as possible to use this book to be inclusive of women from a variety of nationalities, sexualities, and religions, but it cannot be overlooked that I will never truly know these struggles on the same scale that women of color and women of other religions and sexualities do. While I hope to be a safe space for all women, the absence of women of color and LGBTQIA+ women in all artistic mediums is an issue that deserves our attention and I would like to take a moment to recommend the following poets whose work I greatly admire:

Renee Gladman
Lang Leav
Tania Hart
Alycia Pirmohamed
Mai C. Doan
Layli Long Soldier

Thank you to Annelise Argent, for helping me develop a platform for my work. Thank you to Candice Mac for bringing to life my vision for the cover, and for doing it with such enthusiasm. Thank you to Kangwa for sharing such beautiful words to open this collection. Thank you to Amy Loynd for helping edit and proofread.

Thank you to Mom and Dad for giving me $5 for my first writing competition, for being my first sponsor when I started making history content and for believing in me when I couldn't. Thank you to my sister, brother-in-law and my brothers. Thank you to my dearest friends who have eagerly read and supported my poems along the way. Thank you to the love of my life, for showing me that the love I've read in pages exists in this world. Thank you to my teachers and professors, for giving me the tools and the rule books and promptly encouraging me to break them. Thank you to the people who've given me an audience in readings or for my little history ramblings on social media.

And to you, reader, whose eyes are flitting across the words before you. Thank you.

I am no Helen.
No legions of gilded warships will scour the sea for Me.

I am no Boudica.
No armies of blood angry men will gather and wilt for Me.

I am no Marie.
No honor of reverent awards will garnish the grave for Me.

Yet I have sent out a thousand ships for You.
And faced down the armies of hell for You.
And given my nights shrouded in questions
For You.

Quietly,
Stubbornly,
On my "only."

Because I am a woman.
And that's just what we do.
Simply, I am a woman.
Is that not enough?
For Me

For You

Amy Loynd

Sappho

In tombstone parchment
my love, we lay you down.

I, scribe to your sepulchre
you, angel to my shoulder.

Your spirit takes any form
the reader could maladapt.

A soldier in silver heart,
a husband not his own,

A lady richer or poorer,
under veil and incense.

But they will never see
how she appeared to me.

Joan of Arc

Never enough sermons whispered aloud
or prayers shouted under foggy breaths
could save a world rusting into apathy
and burning alive into anarchy.

I never feared the flames,
but being the only one left behind
to sweep away the ashes.

Olga of Kyiv

Salt clinging to my lashes,
lips biting into cracks,
grinding enamel to gums,
fingernails digging into dermis,
ribs aching as lungs expand.
You've cried a throat bloody.
Embers rooted in your feet
pulsate a once fledgling pyre,
and it reignites a second time.
You're not dead yet, my love.
Burn them to the pits hell,
and start building again.

Matoaka

They have sewn her name onto lifetimes,
but never the one that she truly lived.

Ahone created her in the water's tide,
man stole her in baptismal fonts.

Are not the spirits of heaven the ones
who are meant to curse the land?

Has man surpassed the wrath of gods,
great Oki now crushed under boots?

They preferred the simple taste of home,
and shared the recipe she never ate.

When the taste of her being was bitter,
they traded in her foreign syllables.

Frances Ellen Watkins Harper

In hissing meadow glens
where a shepherd's pride
rests in woolen paradise
with nary evil inklings.

The very same olive tree
under which Christ bled
sits the dove on its twigs
warming eggs underwing.

Mankind to rule the beast
that only raises her claws
to feast, protect, defend.
Alas, we are not equals.

Because how can a man
look upon his own kin
and imagine they'd suit
manacles better instead?

While man has his faults,
you fall short of the word.
Are you not ashamed to be
undermined by animals?

Dora Gordine

Garlick-a-tick, scraped the pick
through clays and bronze heads.
The beautiful are tiresome to me,
I cannot chip beauty in symmetry.

With locks twirled round my ears
braiding Estonia, Latvia, Russia.
Weaving tansy with bare fingers,
original sins in Richmond linger.

Mouths and nostrils are nothing,
how do I ever pencil in your soul?
My Hare, you were pink and blue,
we weren't love, but we were true.

This house was once a promise
that we had survived the thieves.
With artist's hands, brick by brick
like his bust I carved tick-a-tick.

When blinded they took-a-took
your golden cup and my bronze.
Recovered maybe, but no return
on promised survival we'd earned.

Light the cigarette, unzip the bag,
and burn every tree but the apple.
Over bass, can you hear a sigh?
I want my own bed, one last time.

Mary Wollstonecraft

The river welcomed me more
than men's arms ever could.
Old chalked stone crumbling
under foot far more steady.
"Lost woman found drowned"
they'll iron in morning news
on Roman fonts and keys.
Lunatic hysteria in cottons
without the decency to die
in lace and silk stockings.
A man should've kept her,
plucked out green feathers
then gild for golden locks.
She'll lay speckled eggs
and chew on her talons,
sing songs for his friends.
But he flies away by day.
His wings span the skies,
full extensions beyond bars.
If I can pick away the lock,
I'll fly away to the bridge
before they catch my tail.

I didn't want a whole sky,
Just a branch to call mine.
But they couldn't let me.
Each cloud was spoken for.
The vacant ones reserved
for anyone but the hen.
But the wind and the water
eddy and whistle at my call.
I shall ruffle your coattails,
you will drink from my dregs,
parch your sins in the scarlet,
and then ask her for seconds.
The winds from the bridge
embracing me welcome.
Come home safely, dear.

Cleopatra

Entangled in stone snows and green grows
Twirling ribbons of red at a hemmed skirt
A pair of weathered boots across acres tow
One two three, step to thee, swift and curt.

They spilt golden wine down the wall's edge
And silver chalices tinkered against the gate
Like a misshapen lock past its use and bent
When a furtive keykeeper attends too late.

And night sounds like a devilish clock's tick
With moonlight splashing slithering scales
Winding amidst Roman daggers and tricks
Confessing crumb clues of poisoned trails

Her lavender perfume soaking in a vial
Entwined with crimson venom unspent
The silver locket swinging all the while
A hanging noose splashed in lovers' scent.

This world has kept all its secrets hidden
And theirs is one unknown but long-told
The end known to all but furtive two within,
when sin tastes like a dance on stones of old.

Manche Masemola

When hearing a loving Father whisper to
her while on her knees and assure: 'Thou'rt true.
Doubt not that there's a plan for my work to do,
and my love for you shall never fall through!'

Then would she rise, brace herself, and thrive,
ironed free the wrinkles of deliberate sin;
fully submerged into Piety's noble life
and willed and molded to go entirely in.

Yet not so. Humanity is destined to fail.
Why must we stand once more to recede?
Futile Folly opens a trapdoor to a new jail,
and venomous Envy casts seeds of Greed.
Oblivious Huddled Masses ignore her wail
and skirt around all the puddles she bleeds.

Nellie Bly

It took so little
for you to think
me mad.

Help. Me.

Just as little
as little girls
can do.

Help. Me.

Bellevue eyes,
a mystery waif,
ice flesh.

Help. Me.

Positively mad,
a lovely lunatic,
Stunt girl.

Help. Me.

Rosenhan maids
digging in waste,
tied down.

Help. Me.

Now I'm set free,
she's sane as me.
Still trapped.

Help. Her.

Ana Mendieta

I'm sorry that spilling my blood
made you feel uncomfortable.
Sew back together the trousers
you cut off with kitchen scissors
and I'll be dressed in a moment.

Will you help me untie my hands
so I can wash up after dessert?
I'll sweep away all the feathers,
I'm sure I left that chicken head
lying around here somewhere...

If you don't like the pictures,
rip the frames off of the nails.
I should know better than that,
than painting irrigation veins
that made you feel insecure.

It's my mistake for using paint
in the shade loony Cuban red
when you preferred white walls.
Give me a push on my way out,
how could I do it without you?

Catherine II of Russia

All the curtsies, power and success in
the foot of my bed.

But you'll never see me as anything more
than a daughter.

And you'll never see me as anything less
than a disappointment.

I'm the most regretful gift God can bestow
upon a mother.

The set of skirts that kept you from what
you dreamt you deserved.

Marie Antoinette

A child painted like a royal lady
with no chance of being a child.
Running barefoot through a field
flashing the whites of soft soles
and laughing as juvenile lambs.
But she faces bare the crowds,
and the kisses mutate into jeers,
they spit, gnash, claw, scream.
The priceless juvenile mourns,
though far away as they were
with lily feet and golden wheat
worth more than jeweled armor
and hoped she would see again.
She could never afford it now,
they stole away the last of her.

Artemisia Gentileschi

It is true, you'd assume,
paints are without words.
Letters have they none,
the canvases sing octaves.
But we commision not for
their foreign languages.
My fluency has wasted.

It is true, that a muse
could a prodigy make,
but clays and pigments
bend and brush in hand
of one who lights flame
and fingers tips of gore
that becomes a master.

It is true, Susanna cried,
as they pulled her hair.
True again by candles
that Judith did laundry
after Abra assisted her
in curing the headache
that plagued Holofernes.

It is true, a handkerchief
can muffle your screams,
but a jury is as effective
as deafness after a blow.
Silence echoes loudest.
Have you listened at all,
or were your ears askant?

It is true, I never claimed
that I'm born without bile.
I have stolen into sheets,
shifted coins into pockets,
but I never trifled with life
as much as I willed paints
to color the skies above.

It is true, thumbscrews
can steal away the gift
of an artist's livelihood.
But it is true that death
would be less frightful
than to share breaths
in a world same as you.

It is true that the father
is surpassed by his son
laying claim to estates,
titles and heavy names.
They are his from birth.
Yet he seems to forget
he has a daughter, too.

Mary Tudor

Such a short little reign
marked in boiling blood.

Missing a puzzle piece
floating in Channel seas.

Sorry you didn't like it,
not that it matters now.

I was just following in
my father's footsteps.

Jane from Jamestown

A foolproof recipe for powdered wife!
Suitable for winter nights. Serves 6.
Mash potato and parsnip and boil.*
Grind one handful of fresh herbs
and set aside.

Roast meat over flame for an hour
until desperate or tender to taste.
Just a pinch of salt and supper's sorted.
Such a delicacy as I've never had!
Is it a family recipe?

Your neighbors will claw down the door
for leftovers. Even better the next day!
Isn't that the best thing about the settlers?
They know how to use
every bit of the girl.

**(Other roots may be substituted)*

Frida Kahlo

My soles bared to the grass
and cloaked under dying sun
I curved along the forest path
where I found one. A feather!

As blue as the royalty's down,
soft to touch as velvet robes
and as light as the crown will
weigh heavy on steady mind.

Pressed between fingertips,
walking under guarding trees,
lay another, then two, four, six,
an even dozen plumage gems.

Soldier poppy red, yellow gold,
magentas, violets, awaiting me.
My luck, my fortune grows fast!
I'll lay my skin on a colored bed.

Coins counted and wealth bled,
white silk skirts clinging to dirt,
ice breeze demanding posture
for the new minor-key melody.

All visions of prosperity erased
when I saw her lamenting here,
the songbird of beautiful blues,
with a beak-gaped ajaw in song.

But with staccato fallen loose,
she wailed down to the heavens,
ripped a feather from her breast,
and flapped the next pitiful post.

A mourning sigh to silent diety,
and cries wrenched to devils,
her next feather she wrenched
with prayer, she can no longer fly.

The emerald fell with diamonds
and the collection I buried upon
when at last her wings voided,
was peace when flight ended.

Mary Seacole

Oh, poor little doll!
What ails you today?
Is it a plague caught
from Kingston town?
Rest your head down,
and angle your legs up.
Trust her, she learned
from the very best.

Oh, poor young pup!
Did you need shelter?
She'll build up a home
with driftwood scraps.
Mother built this place,
the other inn was full.
She'll open her door,
and call you her son.

Oh, poor wee woman!
Do you not feel alone?
Dread of night journey,
her blood flows along.
Can not both day and
night share a throne?
She'd call you a sister,
but you'd call her other.

Oh, you poor husband!
Once more, another try?
She'll restore spasms
to the heart she craved.
She grinds with knuckles
herbs grown at home.
She'd bring some back,
but she travels a widow.

Oh, you poor reader!
How did you forget her?
She saw neither enemy
nor foe among their faces.
Then the world determined
that she was among them.
And the same world said
"I've never heard of her."

Catherine I of Russia

I was born into stark nothing
but molded into everything.

You cowered before his fist,
he'd rest his head in my lap.

They begged for ink drops,
yet I barely wrote my name.

Excess inflated my lungs
and left you privy to hell.

Did you kill for a throne?
All I had to do was to live.

Charlotte Corday

Angels, unlike vampires,
never beg for a welcome.
Do kiss my sister goodbye,
and paint my cheeks red
under the stinging palms.

Blood emptied of its veins
courses in search of trails.
Did they fail to report that
his flaky skin had pruned
before my knife slid into?

Crimson curled in the bath
onto the white linen blouse.
Father, forgive my passing
as you forgave those sons
who slaughtered daughters.

Lilith

A woman sculpted in same dirt
from nigh you drew first breath
could never satiate your piety.

You never did savor the mirror,
and you called it vanity when I
stole a glance and admired it.

I just wanted to see what gift
our Father bestowed and yes,
it was beauty to Earth anew.

Should I never look at a gift?
In the pond ripples she's here.
Must I never have drink again?

In the darkness of your eyes,
a woman looks back into mine.
Shall I cast my eyes to the soil?

And see that you buried my bed
with she who would always obey
and never taste nature's flesh.

Eve

Seek through xylophone ribs
and you'll find there a woman
with downcast eyes.

However could she sculpt
Promethean clays of gods
without the fruit?

You drank from her blood
in the womb of her making.
She loved you.

Foolish woman, you gave
away Paradise for nectar.
Tear your flesh.

Every woman suffers you,
though the long branch has
two apples missing.

The Six Wives of Henry VIII

Humble and loyal I remained
until my muscles atrophied.
A doctor's scalpel nicked out
a widow of a heart blackened,
your name stitched in thread,
the very pattern of your shirts.

The most happy I'd have been
with her little soul in my arms.
And the most fury you had felt
when our dear daughter smiled
and reached out her tiny palms
only for you to slap them away.

Bound to obey and serve you
for how else should I behave
with a swinging axe overhead?
They will call it love, devotion
without knowing goose flesh
when your voice raises pitch.

God send me well to keep you
in the finest of silks and wools
with your hands tangled gold
other bodices and under skirts.
Find your affections anywhere,
anywhere where I will never be.

No other will but his, they sang,
from the moment I lay my head.
The will of teachers, of stewards,
and the willful whims of a king
who dreams of roses, after all,
my own dream is treasonous.

To be useful in all that I do, do
you listen to my soul's whisper?
I let the patters of my heart die
to preserve our own bits of flesh.
In that closet I affixed my duty,
but what else I'd do if I could!

Idia

"My son," she says, "though you've departed my womb,
you will always have a mother with you."

"My son," she prays, "by a miracle you were given to me.
See to it that you waste no opportunities."

"My son," she guides, "remember the righteousness in rage.
As Oba, it is your birthright to rampage."

"My son, she chides, "a dance can conquer as much as war,
but if you stumble, consider what for."

"My son, she warns, "don't lose your face to the thieves.
They will pillage and pick us clean."

"My son," she's sworn, "raise all my grandchildren as strong
as the women who before you came along."

Lucretia

You kept her as your war spoils
rage and pillage her barricades
and laid barren the cannon fires
with her final defense to drown.

Her nails carved into her retinas,
her teeth guillotined the tongue,
Her nasal cartilage lay pulverized,
against last witness coral trees.

A tidal painted in cherry waves
an idol desecrated of its senses.
They would not touch her sight
She rescinds her taste and scent.

The spear shrieked out melody
along xylophones of vertebrae
with steel of far more affection
than his hands could ever carry.

Death's scythe sheathed cold
etched through flesh conches
so your putrid words collapse
on her dead ears in the sand.

Sockets emptied, bloody tears
with her sapphires slain to rest
in empty oyster shells coffins.
Now all left to sign the painting.

You tore her arms out of place
before you'd lose a prize bounty
And grimaced upon her own gore.
"So this was their great beauty?"

Juana I of Castile

An entire tabletop bounty of pomegranate seeds
Yet I'm forbidden to crush the pulp under my jaw.

I was always better at advancing through leaves,
and your jealousy decided to saw away my seat.

Through familial foliage, I can see we share eyes
but why is your vision so different on your branch?

A miracle it must be that I maintained my sanity
despite sharing my table and tree with monsters.

Boudica

You can peel my skin inch by inch from sinew,
aim stones at my bones to complete my tomb,
spread my wings in flight and nail them down,
strike matches on my teeth, I'll swallow flames
and let the strays lap up my bubbling corpus.

I would've accepted a martyr's gentle legacy,
but the second you glance at my daughters,
milk of human tolerance curdles in my breast.
If you most fear what havoc man can wreak,
meet a woman who can take nothing more.

Vera Brittain

The light grows quietly
Under the no-man's-land poppies.

Plucked out of snow.
Out of it!

"My dear, have you been there?"
I ask.

"Do you know?"

Elizabeth Fry

An angel among treachery
taking refuge in the straw,
but a demon any man be
when stomachs twist raw.

Have the guards fed you?
They'll remember tomorrow
when they cart you through
the Tyburn's neck to borrow.

Hereditary sins from the Eve
spread to my mother's babe,
there is no soul left to grieve
where a torn chest lies agape.

When cost of death is light,
what value is left for a life?

Procula

"Innocence!" I cried, "Innocence!"
There is no crime greater than innocence.

Confidence, we spoke, in confidence.
You told me you agreed with me in confidence.

"Penitence", I offered, "Penitence."
"Set Him free to exemplify to them penitence."

"Capital offense!" They cheered, "Capital offense!"
"Crucify Him! To promote peace is a capital offense!"

"Frankincense," he sighed, "Frankincense."
"I'll purify my bloody hands with frankincense."

"Defense?" I wondered, "Defense?"
What hope is there for us if Christ has no defense?

Lady Jane Grey

The skies look full of muslin
Winds wailing through skirts.
They all wanted to command.
Man is created in God's sight
and under God's sight wither.
I don't mind giving this away,
crowns caused me headaches.

May I please go home now?

Beatrix Potter

There rolls the stone again
Down another distant hill
With no moss to tempt her.

Into slowing to a stop
Hot air blows to thwart her
She stutters and flickers.

Yet the pressure of gravity
Shoves her forward and leaves
A chilling winter in her wake.

Vines and rotting red leaves
Threaten entanglement,
And return to the garden.

An edition nouvelle
supplants an increasingly dull
and soiled collection.

Caterina Sforza

Taking your little threats on my chin
makes it hard to keep my grimace
from laughing aloud.

Clasping a hand over my mouth
won't erase the curses I mutter
into your palms.

Slamming the door against my nose
doesn't deter me from reaching
for the handle.

Hiking my skirts up to my brows,
I exposed myself to the pitchforks.
Take them *all*.

Annie Besant

You speak a language I have studied,
but cannot practice aloud
because the sound of
my voice is too
grating.
But I refuse to
let rust eat my lips,
I must exercise my jaw
before it locks into complacent quiet.
To be fed isn't generous
when it's to avoid
the hassle of
corpses.
Is my body
not better used
on the pyre aflame
than stuffed with tubes
with a spirit churning in damp gruel.
Soaked bread will drown
out her militancy,
her rebellion.
Never.

Mai Ziadeh

She sits with poison
swelling in her breast.
And her children cry,
"Mama, we're hungry!"
If they feed, they perish,
But if she preserves
her modesty,
Their insides strangle
And devour themselves.

Dora Richter

We last heard her begging,
"Throw me to the dogs,
not to the male yard.
There's only so much
that dogs can do
to me."

We still do not know
to whom they fed her.

Elisabeth Dmitrieff

They assumed
Colors
Are not important.
But look!
What I can offer
to the canvas.
Splash red
and there's
Revolutsia!
And scraps of
Aquinas!
Frate!
Und alle as well...

Noor Inayat Khan

She cannot delicately type words
that carry messages of grief.

Nor will she sit on her hands
when she can clasp yours.

Nothing scares them more
than opening your fists

And letting fall the jewelry
ripped from our necks.

If she is not suited to jump,
then let the wind carry her!

An elephant cannot claim
the birthright of owls.

With liberty on her lips,
she will soar instead.

Pingyang

"What is going on?" Asked the child to his grandfather.
"A leader has died." Words swirling over jade grandeur.

"How did the leader die?" Steps turn to dust red clay.
"The *hun* flies free, as mine and yours will one day...

To the white of the moon swirling porcelain ripples in tides,
rattling empty filial bowls until it smells the earth of the hillsides.

Po admires the bronze like a purring cat, curling into bones.
Hun and *po* meet as friends after conquest in their new home.

Beasts guard the bed carved with horses and dragons
and nominal silks atop black and gold lacquered wagons."

"What makes them cry, Grandfather?" Flutes crying to doves.
"Because they loved, child. We give paradise for those we love."

Seventy thousand footsteps marching through ripples of gold
Paying last honors in *sancai* glazes to protect their protector tenfold.

"How did the leader die?" Golden horns wailing, mourning.
"As a leader lives, for their people." Rested face with muslin adorning.

"He must have been a great warrior to die for our cause."
"Yes," the band's breath falls, and his lips wrinkle wider "*she* was..."

Gentile Budrioli

Are your hands warmed now
at her funeral pyre?
Did her cremated bones give
crunch underfoot?
Don't waste her bubbling fat,
save it for the stew.
Waxy flesh melts off sinews
like candle from cord.
What was she meant to tell them?
Final words for quills.
She wishes you nothing more than well.
They wish for her deepest depths of Hell.

La Malinche

Loyalty of the flower buds
to the shining sun above
and dedication of the bees
to the pollen of the pistols
honey sweet to the tongue.

But the flowers never wove
a caging vine around a star
and swallowed wings first
The creature who thought
only to make nectar pure.

So what rays can she give
when there are only storms
that have swarmed inside.
How do your flowers hold
against her pointing finger?

Scratched nail beds in grass,
one line in heroism, golden
one traitorous, silver shone.
Her screams will lullaby you
regardless of where she steps.

Eleanor of Aquitaine

Fogged whispers across the bogs
your soldiers trembled upon logs
of she who shreds your jaw agog
and drown the seas mid-epilogue.

Sentences fail all my recompense.
My unrepentant remorselessness
strangling 'round a widow in chest
Still cries louder than his abscess.

My effigy never mortal sleep implies,
the shadows follow blackest night.
In restlessness, I'll not allow to die
the fire that warms, burns, defies.

Remissed be, if I wouldn't promise
that no story is as dark an abyss
as my shadow in the pretty flesh
when I withhold your death's kiss.

Rosalind Franklin

When I raise my hand to speak,
They check my manicure and ring.
When he raises his hand, they listen.

When they turned the questions around,
I had to shout to be heard.
All they had to do was whisper.

When they interrupted an idea,
I pursed my lips and bowed my head.
They're offered apologies and attention.

When I repeated myself after being misheard,
I was called troublesome, emotional.
When they repeat themselves, it is

dramatic emphasis.

Riding my coattails, they wore medals on their chests.
I'm remembered in hindsight at best,
when I changed the world.

Jael

You endured your suffering like a woman?
He means to say that he languished
with the marrow sucked from his bones
and wailing trailing air from his lungs.

But to know suffering like a woman
is to be acquainted with silence,
to walk in cold flesh that others
will carve initials with blunt stares.

Feel the ache in your temple,
imagine a phantom fang embeds
and when you whisper of your pains,
they scream out of your madness.

But even as we stretch the stakes
and take a life to save our sons,
should my skirts shift ever so much
they'll color my visage wanton.

But no need to dwell on our suffering.
My sins were made in sacrifice
but inside your skull is your portrait
which marks your seat in flames.

Lyudmila Pavlichenka

Ready.

His open neck rained blood on the tree.

Wouldn't a soldier be better served by
Taut skirts that flash toned flesh thigh?

Aim.

I opened my mouth, desperate, thirsty.

Add a mirror company onto a rifle scope
To touch up your lipstick in a cold moat.

Squeeze.

My husband's murderer makes a fine drink.

Your rations might be a gram too generous,
A prisoner's diet helps you fit that dress!

Fire.

For peace, a fascist's life is an affordable fee.

Shouldn't a soldier be a far prettier sight?
Fan my skirt to hide them. Let women fight.

Audre Lord

Every step with
every woman.

Their voices
lullabies her.

She alone cannot
change anything?

But she alone walks
with an army.

They beg her,
give me a name!

She'd give anything
to say a word,

How can you not
use your voice

When silence
is what kills?

When you, who
shares a struggle

with your sisters,
also turns away,

must they fight you
as they fight for you?

When you perform
in front of mirrors

and whisper slurs
behind the door.

Align her name
front to back

and see the trees
that grew behind her.

Marsha P. Johnson

Wouldn't it be luxurious to be known?
With stars engraved to call your own?
To rile crowds with brags to riches
And fuel beliefs of their ambitions.

With change sparkling in her pockets,
And love listed on charging dockets,
Her shirts creasing inside rucksacks,
They map a city anew from her back.

When their friends slip down the trails
and behind the smile to tragedy unveil
legends so often find themselves alone
and only noted after the carved stone.

Shireen Abu Akleh

While the raining blue shrapnel dust
Scraped the clear flesh out her eyes
And needles filled our gasping lungs,
her back flattened against a screen.

Hot glass with hot pixilated rainbows,
There's a family there! She is saved!
Someone can see what they've done!
Jaws agape in yawns, they stretch.

Reclining, they fix their eyes on her
And fiddle plastic with rubber buttons.
What will give way first? Her red fists?
Or the wall that keeps them from her?

Her screams give him a bloody headache.
This is too depressing to watch first thing
He contemplates, lying at her broken feet
while sands shift and pile into eardrums.

I like the noise, she says, looking down,
It helps me focus on my work, she says
It's good to know what's going on there,
She says while her brush scrapes canvas.

Acidic bemusement floods her stomach
And splits the cracks of glass fractures
In all her charred appendages scattered.
We still know, and can sleep peacefully.

Hypatia

The wolves in metal helmets
stuck their snouts in linens
soiled by their oiled hands.
Smothered the same tribon,
which hems you tongued
as I cried aloud to the air.
My skull could be drowning
in golden treasures, yet
they'd never look inside
if the neck attached wasn't
silken under their calluses
and the legs at right angles.

Mahapajapati Gotami

In a world with leaders aplenty,
courage lies in following first.
When a branch burns aflame,
green foliage smokes greatest.

In a world of guardians galore,
what truly makes one a mother?
Is it the birth alone on linen beds,
or the soul cradling a child close.

In a world of mantras, testaments,
faith comes from a feast of hope.
As certain as the yellow sun rises,
we die and are born day after day.

Caroline Norton

Pink roses pinched between his thumb
green straw cracking under knuckles
when he asked for her hand and soul.

"I shall wear it in my hair!" She cried
and tucked it into her obsidian plaits.
"No," he insisted, "on your bodice."

The rose resting on her collar lace
drew eyes to the petals, but thorns
chafe in both insertion and removal.

"I shall tell my friends!" She replied
and drew the quill from the desk.
"No," he protested, "say not a word."

Sorrowful Rosalie, what shall you do?
Had he written your story, they'd know,
and send him notes for the damages.

"I shall hold our children!" She sighed
and curled empty arms to her breast.
"No," he resisted, "they bear my name."

If Eve orphaned from Abel and Cain,
while Adam watched Cain kin slain,
would she too not a stranger become?

"I shall stand and let them all see."
While the brushes bruises masked.
"Yes," another assisted, "My Justice."

Christine de Pizan

I'll pray to saints and goddesses
for my intact skirts and bodices
not unwoven under their palms
hungrily cupping my flesh alms.

Lacy brides a tasty morsel makes
To fill her husband's supper plates.
Vows such a terror in me instilled
when uttered in spite of thy will.

Yet what beauty can love inspire
when twin candles match desire.
How I'd sooner be free with thee
than wealthier with he and lonely.

Yaa Asentwa of Ghana

With two arms she'll spin webs sparkling
yet she can carry the load of eight of you.
For she'll walk with gold under her feet,
where once glass peeled soles like yams.
She will weave and sit and make her nest.
Of course, she knows death, but of course
you will see her until the existence ends.

Sacagawea

This way,
follower, follower.
They take her across mountains.

This way,
follower, follower.
He pays for her life with coins.

This way,
follower, follower.
A child curls against her spine.

This way,
follower, follower.
He calls her by an easier name.

This way,
follower, follower.
Her footsteps set tracks and rails.

Follow her.
Follow her.
Follow her.
Follow her.

Gabriela Mistral

Time and Death are sisters.
Time and Death are co-workers.
Time unravels knots of scarlet silk
and Death's little hand hovers,
waiting to collect the spool.

Time, the golden girl from birth,
we kiss her feet, lick her soles.
We frame her on our walls.
We wear her on our wrists.
But who likes to think of Death?

When we speak of her, hushes fall,
and they interrupt her sentences.
We paint our talk a lighter color.
"It gets dark so early now."
"Oh! Would you look at the time!"

Mythology writes Death wretched,
with dripping fangs and green breath.
But Death, her lovers cheat her.
Death postpones her dates.
Who among men can outrun Time?

Death is the nightwatch, Time hunts.
She giggles and sprints to your left.
She races endless during joy,
slowly bleeds during despair.
Oh! Would you Look at the time!

Everyone prays Death loses her way,
But they beg on knees Time to stay.
Do you have the time?
Just one minute, hour, day more!
Oh! Would you look at the time!

Time goes and Death collects scraps.
Almost always they pathetically beg,
I have never loved greater than Time!
But when they wish for Death...
Oh. Would you look at the time!

Virginia Brindis de Salas

Her heart pulsates morse codes.
A drop of blood from the mothers
who gave their children first breath.

A bead of sweat from Papa's brow,
as he bent under the sun's flames,
finds rest in the wrinkles in her palm.

Saliva swirling around her front teeth
carries the taste of wine in glasses.
Grandpa used to spit out dirty juices.

Grandma's knuckles wove pastel yarns
to wind scarves around cold windpipes.
She used the same bones to splash ink.

A tapestry of habits may have woven
from the centuries before she breathed,
But traditions will evaporate with her.

Alfreda Markowska

The blackened blood
pounding in their ears
drown out heartbeats
beneath draped skirts.
The first snowflakes
in Hell flurry away,
honey trickles, pours
sour on the tongues
before her palms to
vultures would open.
For every branch hewn
From her familial Eden,
She lives another world
An eternity entirely.

Hatshepsut

To grinding her bones into dust is not enough,
burn every word ever slipped through her lips.
Even with her soul orphaned from the corpse,
her name is still at the mercy of their chisels.
And sands eroding the figures down to rivets,
undetectable, unrecognizable to oiled fingers.

The natural world does not spin fast enough
to entrust sands to the most pertinent tasks.
His robes draped her figure, hyperbole lips
and lioness fangs affixed, swallowed earth.
Whether hatred, necessity or eyed vulgarity,
not even a memory could escape their fists.

Wu Zetia

Is her name not lonesome,
written down all by herself?
See the Daughter of Heaven,
they nearly left her shelved.
Is she not ruler of the mouth,
with tongue and teeth knelt?
or does she command the ear,
Like the song of a dagger slice
cleansed over the running silks.
Great names are seen, heard,
tasted, feared, and worshipped
and the ink must be amended
and the name from lips ascend
will curl and stretch like wind
shiver leaves, rattle branches
with the smell of river shores
recalling the titles of bygone
and gooseflesh under a sole
where once her feet bore her.

Eliza Suggs

How the sunshine and a shadow both blind
with daisy petal yellows and oceanic night.
Where Julys scald but the shade holds kind,
So too autumnal rays scratch out grey light.

God's day and dusk made to share heaven
With feathers and hides and oceans below.
Salvation's hiding place on days of seven
And here melodic hymnal rivers doth flow.

When your fingertips trace splintered bark,
after the songbirds beaks close for the day,
Do one's eyes cherish stillness of night dark?
And do starry lights burn our retinas away?

What strength had she to live through Hell,
yet sang through stars for her story to tell!

Julia de Burgos

What do the words of heart read
When the ribcage unfolds stripes?

What notes shall then meet the air
When her jaw hangs peacefully?

What ink stains from imperfect verse
When her palm is lined with fortune?

What thoughts will spill at your feet
When her skull is split against tiles?

What organ releases the soul's respite
When a minute hand stills a quarter till?

What will you say when you find her joy
When you thought you'd picked her clean?

Rani Lakshmlbal

Of all the fruits which one may eat
you'll find nothing tastes so sweet
than nectar of the foe's defeat
or a fate crowned in salvation.

On shoulders do her burdens stack,
she lifts her load where others lack
with worlds of eyes tied to her back
denizen's knees bend for her sword.

When they shed the blood of her kin,
must she shed her tears in doctrine
and let snakes live to shed their skin?
The new regiments bear her name.

Revenge for likewise conduct yearns
for to-be dissenters to forever learn
that rebels are scattered in from urns
But she? She asked to be fed to flames.

Christina Rosetti

Your hands make mine chill
as winds of idle misty March
billowing in an emerald glen.
The hairs on my neck arch.

Against the grounds slap my feet.
My heart pounds in a race
between my body and my soul.
To you, we soar and chase.

The blood, contradictory red
to the blue ice, inside my chest
pumps against a cage of ribs
when I your hand caressed.

A fire from ahead, white demon
drags you away from my side
and into a summery Hell
wherein five months you abide.

I'd give the coat off my back,
let my bare feet touch the snow
if you'd freeze me with you
so from you, I'd never go.

Are you ever coming back?
I hardly see you more than air
except in the cold exhale when I
Feel your arms around me bare.

Ana Nzinga

Wake up, girl, your brother is dead
The poison didn't sit well with him.
Tear the seams from his shoulders,
the robes better suit your frame.

Diplomacy will need translating,
but every tongue knows the spear.
True power lies in being despised
than being adored for meekness.

If you flee, burn your tracks away,
press your heels into his vertebrae.
Line them all up elbow to ribcage,
and free those who they enslaved.

Artemisia I of Caria

In over my heart,
with a level head.

Feet flat grounded,
fists unclenched.

Lips sewn shut,
jaw wide open.

Lungs vacant,
throat filled brim.

Stomach in aches,
eyes at ease.

Knees trembling,
elbows locked.

I am still here,
you have gone.

Khadija bint Khuwaylid

Her eyes rise to the skies with the sun,
golden shining coins to buy salvation.
If wealth's whispers carry on the winds,
what rumors shall your purse say of you?

Her palms extended, the moons prostrate
and shadows bend their tapestry threads.
When a heart is unsettled on their demise,
what pillars can be built to protect them?

Her neck bows down to bid starry sky away
and kiss goodbye to those sorrowful years.
Does power froth and scream for all to hear
or steadily hum in the winds wrapping round?

Josephine Baker

A strange thing, is it not?

Worn on collars like a Goddess
To be worshipped as a Venus,
and painted like a pearl.

Yet you wouldn't eat crumbs
the same table
as her.

A funny joke, is it not?

When she's invited to dine finely
and drink from a crystal glass,
she's a traitor.

How could she turn her back
on a country that turned
on her?

Mary Verghese

She's known the horrors of the world?
She must be rancorous and wretched.

No, she used her pain to know others' pain.

She's a respected leader in her field?
She must retreat to an empty home.

No, love lightened her family doors.

She is a woman of medicine of science?
Clearly she turned her back on our God.

No, her eyes were familiar with the heavens.

She never had any children of her own?
Her selfishness will eliminate her legacy.

No, her name is carved above healing rooms.

So when will you admit to yourselves
in the caverns of your foxed souls
that you hate her for not being
embittered by this world like you.

Evelyn Scott

The oldest child took ten steps on that earth.
The middle child left seven footprints.
The youngest but only three.

That well used to belong to the people she knew.
One day, they shared buckets with strangers,
the next, they made her give a password.

They moved the fenceposts inch by inch in the soil.
The roots tangled on the picket bars.
Behave and you'll be set free.

When they excavate her bucket from the stream
or the children's shoes from the blushing dirt,
will they mispronounce their names?

Maria Josefa Gabriela Silang

Can he abide lies other than victory?
He'd die happily by a man's barrel,
but to perish by a woman's hand?
The same would follow him to Hell.

How could he death approach him
as a being so weak, mindless, ugly?
Those hands meant to please him
powdering her nose with saltpeter.

No, perhaps she was truly a man.
A peek in her trousers will resolve.
Why should he be bent to his knees
just because she planned ahead?

He'd lick the crumbs off the dirt
before he accepted her handouts.
What world can this be if it is she,
she was the better man all along?

Sarah Winnemucca

Two wolves may satiate their hunger within
and gnaw their teeth against the branches,
but the coyote laps up their splintered twigs.

Two wooden fragments lodge into their flesh,
either when the arrows evade from their bows
or thorns await fleeing feet to pierce the soles.

Do you remember when the flowers used sway?
She wore the blooms on her dress and danced.
The breeze rustled petals and pistols triggers.

The mountains pierced the earth's Teton skin
blocking hundreds of promises from sunlight.
They buried the traveler before her summit.

OTMA

Once burned my cheeks pink
to scare away the unknown.
My hat tossed into the ocean
and bobbed under the waves.

Opal palaces and military beds,
tepid baths encrusted in gold
Mama, may I go outside today?
All I want is to make a friend.

Ordinary yolks in crystal shells,
they left us to raise ourselves.
My purse chinks with currency.
Alas, I cannot spend a kopek.

Open a white window to the sky,
the gunfire locks the latch shut.
My nails shred the floorboards.
Are you going to forget me now?

Epilogue

I wish on suns more than anything
That I could've been gentle in this world,
To have Eden innocence in my eyes
And see the best in my neighbors.
But tart nectar turned sour.
Now I cannot see another soul
without wondering what kind of monster
lurks behind the eyelids of his stare.

INDEX

(in chronological order)

Eve

Considered in Christianity as the first woman on earth, she was the wife of Adam and the mother of all humanity. She was often assigned responsibility for eating the forbidden fruit that led to their banishment from the Garden of Eden.

Lilith

According to Jewish legend, she was Adam's first wife made from the same soil as him. She was banished from the Garden of Eden for not being subservient to Adam and turned into a she-demon.

Jael

The heroine of the Battle of Mount Tabor in the Hebrew Bible and the Christian Old Testament. She killed the commander of the Canaanite army by hammering a stake through his skull in the Book of Judges.

Sappho (c. 610–570 B.C.E.)

An Archaic Greek poet from the island of Lesbos, she has been regarded as one of the greatest lyric poets of all time. Most of her poetry today only exists in fragments, but it is believed that she wrote over 10,000 lines.

Mahapajapati Gotami (c. 600– c. 480 B.C.E.)

The aunt and adoptive mother of Siddhartha Gautama, the founder of Buddhism. According to Buddhist tradition, she was the first woman to request ordination and became the first bhikkuni, or Buddhist nun.

Lucretia (d. 510 B.C.E.)

An ancient Roman noblewoman whose story has fallen into mythohistory. Following her rape at the hands of Sextus Tarquinius, she plunged a dagger into her heart, which is portrayed in various works of art throughout the Renaissance.

Artemisia I of Caria (c. 5th century B.C.E.)

Queen of Halicarnassus, she commanded ships during the naval battles of Salamis and Artemisium and allied with King Xerxes of Persia.

Cleopatra (c. 69–30 B.C.E.)

One of the most identifiable women in history, she was the last active ruler of the Ptolemaic dynasty of Ancient Egypt. Despite her political prowess and intelligence, she is most remembered for her love affairs with Julius Caesar and Mark Anthony and her suicide.

Boudica (30–61)

Queen of the Iceni tribe in Ancient Britain. When Roman forces annexed her late husband's kingdom into their territory, they flogged her and raped her daughters. In retaliation, she led uprisings against the Roman forces until her death.

Procula (d. 81)

Believed to be the wife of Pontius Pilate, who intervened on Christ's behalf during her husband's judgment in the New Testament. She has been canonized as a saint in the Eastern Orthodox Church.

Hypatia (d. 415)

An Alexandrian philosopher, mathematician, and astronomer. Her adherence to Neoplatonism during a time of religious upheaval resulted in her murder at the hands of a Christian mob.

Khadija bint Khuwaylid (c. 556–619)

The first wife of the Prophet Muhammad, the founder of Islam. Often referred to as the "Mother of Believers", she used her wealth as a merchant to support her husband in his prophethood.

Wu Zetia (624–705)

Empress Consort and later Dowager Empress of China during the Tang Dynasty. Under her reign, China's economy thrived and the country became one of the great powers of the world.

Pingyang (c. 589–623)

A princess and general during the time of transition from the Siu dynasty to the Tang dynasty in China. She was the first female general of the Tang dynasty and she was given the funeral rites of a high general.

Olga of Kyiv (c. 890–969)

The regent of the Kyivan Rus and a saint in the Eastern Orthodox Church, she was the first ruler of the Kyivan Rus to convert to Christianity. She is most famous for her brutal retaliation against the Drevlians following the murder of her husband.

Eleanor of Acquitaine (1122–1204)

The Duchess of Aquitaine, Queen of France and then Queen of England, she was one of the most powerful women of the High Middle Ages. She was mother of two of England's most famous kings, the venerated Richard I and the frowned-upon King John.

Queen Idia (15th century)

Mother of Esigie, the Oba of the Edo people in modern-day Benin. The Oba Ozoula married her after seeing her dance. She has been described as a great warrior who led an army to defend her son's right to rule.

Christine de Pizan (1364–1431)

A French-Italian poet who acted as a court writer for King Charles VI of France. She was commissioned by figures such as Philip the Bold and Duke Louis I of Orleans. She is best known for her works *The Book of the City of Ladies* and *The Treasure of the City of Ladies*.

Joan of Arc (c. 1412–1431)

The patron saint of France, she believed she heard the voice of God and was instructed to offer her aid to the dauphin of France during the Siege of Orleans in the Hundred Years' War. She was captured by Burgundian forces and convicted of heresy, being sentenced to death by burning at the stake.

Caterina Sforza (1463–1509)

An Italian noblewoman and alchemist, she acted as regent of Forlì and Imola. One of her first acts as regent was to avenge her husband's death and she had all involved in his death imprisoned and their belongings distributed to the poor.

Juana I of Castile (1479–1555)

Also known as Joana the Mad, she was queen of Castile and Aragon, but under the order of her father, she was kept confined in a palace and declared insane. When her son ascended the throne, he continued to keep her confined and ordered none to speak to her.

Catherine of Aragon (1485–1536)

First wife of King Henry VIII of England and mother of Queen Mary I of England. After more than twenty years of marriage, Henry had her banished from court away from her daughter while he pursued marriage with Anne Boleyn.

Gentile Budrioli (d.1498)

An Italian astrologist and scholar, she studied at the University of Bologna. She maintained exceptional skill as a healer, but lead to her being accused of witchcraft, even by her own husband. She was hanged and then burned alive.

La Malinche or Malintzin (c. 1500–1529)

A Nahua woman who was enslaved and gifted among other slaves to Hernán Cortés and his men. Due to her language skills, she acted as an interpreter and advisor for the Spaniards as they went on to conquer the Aztec Empire.

Jane Seymour (c. 1508–1537)

The third wife of King Henry VIII of England and mother of King Edward VI of England. She married Henry eleven days after the execution of his second wife, Anne Boleyn. Jane was the only one of Henry's wives to receive a queen's funeral.

Anne Boleyn (c. 1509–1536)

The second wife of King Henry VIII of England and mother of Queen Elizabeth I of England. She was sentenced to death on trumped of charges of adultery and treason and was beheaded by sword at the Tower of London.

Katherine Parr (1512–1548)

The sixth and final wife of King Henry VIII of England, she also published various books on religion including *Prayers or Mediations* and *The Lamentation of a Sinner*.

Anne of Cleves (1515–1557)

The fourth wife of King Henry VIII of England, Anne was disparaged after their meeting as being fat and ugly despite contemporary reports to the contrary. Eventually, she agreed to an annulment of their marriage. Following the annulment, Henry referred to her as the "King's Beloved Sister."

Catherine Howard (c.1524–1542)

The fifth wife of King Henry VIII of England, she was wed to the middle-aged Henry as a teenager. She was later convicted of adultery and practiced kneeling before the chopping block the night before her execution.

Mary Tudor / Mary I of England (1516–1558)

Queen of England and Ireland, she was the daughter of King Henry VIII and Catherine of Aragon. She was famously known by the nickname "Bloody Mary" due to the death of nearly 300 Protestants during her reign.

Lady Jane Grey (1537–1554)

An English noblewoman who took the throne of England for less than two weeks, earning her the nickname "Nine Days' Queen". She was eventually overthrown by her cousin, Mary Tudor, and beheaded on the grounds of the Tower of London.

Ana Nzinga (1583–1663)

Also known as Queen Nzinga Mbande, she was a ruler of the Ndongo and Matamba kingdoms of Angola. Experienced in both political and military matters, she stood against the Portuguese during their efforts to establish a colony.

Artemisia Gentileschi (1593–1653)

An Italian painter who painted famous women from mythology and biblical scenes, she was the first woman to join Accademia di Arte del Disegno. She also famously testified, despite being tortured, against her rapist during a grueling trial.

Jane from Jamestown (c.1595– c.1610)

The name granted to the remains found by archaeologists in Jamestown of an English teenage girl. Markings on her bones show that she was a victim of cannibalism during the period of the Jamestown Settlement known as the "Starving Time".

Matoaka (c. 1596–1617)

Also known by the name Pocahontas, she was the daughter of Native American chief Powhatan. She was captured and held for ransom by English colonists before being baptized and given the name Rebecca. She was married to John Rolfe and was presented in English society as a "civilized savage" before she died of illness, possibly smallpox or pneumonia.

Marta Helena Skowrońska / Catherine I of Russia (1684–1727)

A peasant woman of Baltic descent, she was taken prisoner during the Great Northern War where she was given to an advisor of Emperor Peter the Great. She and Peter soon became lovers and then husband and wife and after his death, she succeeded him as empress of Russia.

Catherine II of Russia / Catherine the Great (1729–1796)

Originally a princess of Prussian birth named Sophia Augusta Frederica von Anhalt-Zerbst, she overthrew her husband Emperor Peter III of Russia. She became one of the most recognized figures in Russian history due to her expansion of the Russian empire and her numerous lovers.

Maria Josefa Gabriela Silang (1731 – 1763)
A Filipino military leader who lead the Ilocano independence movement against the colonial powers of Spain following her husband's assassination. Known as the "Joan of Arc of Ilocandia", she was captured by the Spanish with several of her troops and executed by hanging.

Marie Antoinette (1755 – 1793)
Born Maria Antonia of Austria, she married the future Louis XVI of France. Various rumors spread about her during her reign led to her increasing unpopularity. When the royal family was deposed, she was convicted of high treason and beheaded via guillotine.

Mary Wollstonecraft (1759 – 1797)
A British writer and advocate for women's rights, her writings on feminism have been influential for the growing waves of feminism and feminist literature. She was also the mother to author of *Frankenstein*, Mary Shelley.

Charlotte Corday (1768 – 1793)
An active supporter of the Girondins during the French Revolution, she assassinated Jacobin leader Jean Paul Marat in the belief that the revolution would be in jeopardy under his leadership. She was arrested and executed via guillotine.

Elizabeth Fry (1780 – 1845)
A British prison reformer, she advocated for the improvement of prison conditions, particularly for female prisoners. She advocated for the implementation 1823 Gaols Act which separated female and male prisoners. She became known as the "Angel of Prisons".

Sacagawea (c.1788– c.1812)

A Lemhi Shoshone woman, she was kidnapped and sold into marriage at the age of thirteen. She famously went on to aid the navigation of the Lewis and Clark Expedition and has become a symbol of women's value and resilience.

Mary Seacole (1805–1881)

A British nurse of Jamaican ancestry and owner of a boarding house. She was posthumously awarded the Jamaican Order of Merit for her efforts in nursing and housing soldiers during the Crimean War.

Caroline Norton (1808–1877)

An English social reformer and writer, her efforts to gain custody of her children from her abusive husband were instrumental in passing legislation advocating for the rights of women in marriage. She also modeled for Daniel Maclise's *Justice* found in the House of Lords.

Frances Ellen Watkins Harper (1825–1911)

An American writer, abolitionist, teacher, and suffragist, she wrote a large collection of anti-slavery poetry and stories. She was one of the first African American women to publish her written work in the United States. She also aided in the founding of the National Association of Colored Women.

Rani Lakshmlbal (1828–1858)

The consort of Jhansi in the Maratha Empire and a leader of the Indian Rebellion of 1857, she led efforts against the British forces. She died of her wounds sustained in a British attack and her body was cremated so to prevent it from falling into the hands of enemy soldiers.

Christina Rosetti (1830–1894)

British writer, and sister of artist Dante Gabriel Rosetti. Often overlooked in her lifetime, many feminists considered her a symbol of female ingenuity. Her work has also inspired several modern musicians such as Yoko Ono and Bear McCreary.

Yaa Asentwa of Ghana (1840–1921)

Queen Mother of Ashanti Empire ruler Ejisu. She was a key leader in the War of the Golden Stool, a war of independence against the British Empire, by inspiring Ashanti men to take arms against the colonial power of Britain.

Sarah Winnemucca (1844–1891)

A Paiute writer, teacher, and tribal leader, her book *Life Among the Paiutes: Their Wrongs and Claims* was one of the first memoirs published by a Native American woman. She also worked for the Bureau of Indian Affairs as an interpreter and advocated for Native American rights, even lobbying in Washington D.C.

Annie Besant (1847–1933)

A political campaigner and advocate for women's rights, she spoke out in favor of better living conditions and education for the working class. She also became the first president of the Indian National Congress and supported Indian and Irish independence.

Elisabeth Dmirtrieff (1851– c. 1918)

A Russian activist, she helped to found the International Workingmen's Association. She traveled to Paris where she defended the Paris Commune following the end of the Franco-Prussian War, she acted as a key figure for the formation of *L'Union des Femmes*.

Nellie Bly (1864–1922)

An American journalist famous for successfully traveling the world in 72 days, she also wrote an exposé on the conditions of mental asylums and institutions by feigning insanity to observe from the inside. Her efforts paved the way for future investigative journalism.

Beatrix Potter (1866–1943)

An English writer and illustrator, she is most well-known for *The Tale of Peter Rabbit*. Her illustrations of plant samples were widely used in natural science fields. An ardent supporter of land preservation, she left nearly all of her property to the National Trust upon her death.

Eliza Suggs (1876–1908)

An American author and temperance lecturer. Despite having osteogenesis imperfecta and being expected not to live past childhood, she was able to attend classes with the help of her family members and receive a thorough education. She went on to publish a book entitled *Shadow and Sunshine*.

Mai Ziadeh (1886–1941)

A Palestinian-Lebanese writer and translator, she became a renowned figure in the circles of Middle-Eastern literature. She carried the belief that women's emancipation needed to be met with education and representation. After falling into a period of depression, she was placed in a psychiatric hospital by her relatives so they could gain control of her estate.

Dora Richter (1892–1966)

Born in Germany, she was the first woman to receive male-to-female gender-affirming surgery. She was arrested on multiple occasions for wearing women's clothing prior to her surgery and sent to male prisons. She fled to Czechoslovakia during the rise of Nazism in Germany before settling in Bavaria.

Vera Brittain (1893–1970)

An English author and activist, she delayed her education in Oxford to serve as a Voluntary Aid Detachment during World War I. Her memoir *Testament of Youth* detailed her experiences during the war and served as a powerful voice against war.

Dora Gordine (1895–1991)

An Estonian artist and sculptor, she studied art in France and eventually settled in England where she and her third husband, Richard Hare, built Dorich House near Richmond Park. Despite being largely overlooked after her death, she was recognized in her time as one of the finest female sculptors in the world.

Gabriela Mistral (1899–1957)

A Chilean diplomat, teacher, and poet, she worked for Chilean consulates across Europe and participated in cultural communities for the League of Nations. She was the first Latin-American author to receive a Nobel Peace Prize for Literature. Her portrait is featured on the 5,000 Chilean peso bill.

Olga Romanova (1895–1918)

The oldest daughter of Tsar Nicholas II and Alexandra Feodorovna, she would donate from her personal allowances to various charities. She also volunteered as a nurse for a military hospital during World War One. She was killed with her family following the 1917 Russian Revolution.

Tatiana Romanova (1897–1918)

The second daughter of Tsar Nicholas II and Alexandria Feodorovna, she also volunteered as a nurse and acted as chair for a war aid campaign called The Tatiana Committee. She was killed with her family following the 1917 Russian Revolution.

Maria Romanova (1899–1918)

The third daughter of Tsar Nicholas II and Alexandra Feodorovna. She was too young to become a Red Cross nurse like her sisters and instead became the patroness of a military hospital and often visited wounded soldiers. She was killed with her family following the 1917 Russian Revolution.

Anastasia Romanova (1901–1918)

The youngest, and most famous, daughter of Tsar Nicholas II and Alexandra Feodorovna, she was known as the mischievous one of the family. She was killed with her family following the 1917 Russian Revolution. Rumors surrounding whether or not she survived the murder led to her rise in popularity.

Josephine Baker (1906–1975)

An American-born French performer, she was the first black woman to star in a major film, *The Siren of the Tropics*. In addition to her prolific movie career, she assisted with the French resistance movements during World War Two. She was also a Civil Rights Activist and refused to perform for segregated audiences in the United States.

Frida Kahlo (1907–1954)

A Mexican painter famous for her works depicting the intricacies of colonialism and womanhood via her paintings of the natural world and her self-portraits. Her work posthumously reached new heights of fame following the rise of second-wave feminism.

Virginia Brindis de Salas (1908–1958)

A Uruguayan black writer, she is one of the few female poets from Uruguay to have been published. Her writing aimed to bring awareness to the Afro-Uruguayan community and promote equality and social change.

Manche Masemola (1913–1928)

A Pedi woman from Sekhukhuneland or modern-day Johannesburg, she was killed by her parents after converting to Christianity. She is memorialized with a statue of her likeness over the west doors of Westminster Abbey.

Julia de Burgos (1914–1953)

A Puerto Rican poet, journalist, teacher, and avid advocate for Puerto Rican independence. Not only was she elected as Secretary General of the Daughters of Freedom, but she also advocated for African and Afro-Carribean writers.

Noor Inayat Khan (1914–1944)

An Indian-British Special Operations Executive, she participated in an espionage mission to Nazi-Occupied France. Despite the threat of danger, she refused to be evacuated and continued to receive radio signals from England. She was captured and executed in the Dachau concentration camp.

Lyudmila Pavlichenka (1916–1974)

A Soviet sniper during World War II, she joined the war effort when Nazi Germany began its invasion of the Soviet Union. Her number of confirmed kills makes her one of the most accomplished snipers in history.

Rosalind Franklin (1920–1958)

A British scientist whose work in X-ray crystallography was pivotal to the discovery of the structure of DNA. Her contributions went largely unacknowledged and unappreciated during her lifetime as credit was given to Francis Crick, James Watson and Maurice Wilkins.

Mary Verghese (1925–1986)

An award-winning Indian physician, she suffered a spinal

cord injury from a car crash and her own rehabilitation experience led to her making strides in the field of medical rehabilitation and opening the first rehabilitation institute in India. She was the only paraplegic surgeon performing operations during her time.

Alfreda Markowska (1926–2021)

A Polish-Romani woman responsible for saving numerous Jewish and Romani children during the Holocaust and the Porajmos genocides during World War II. She was later awarded the Commander's Cross with Star of the Order of Polonia Restituta.

Evelyn Scott (1935–2017)

An Indigenous Australian activist, she campaigned for the 1967 Constitutional Referendum to recognize indigenous Australians in the official population counts. She acted as leaders of the Federal Council for the Advancement of Aborigines and Torres Strait Islanders and the Council for Aboriginal Reconciliation.

Audre Lord (1943–1992)

An American author, she described herself as a "black, lesbian, mother, warrior, poet" and used her creative works to call out the injustices of racism, sexism, and homophobia. One of her most memorable quotes has been immortalized by a photo of her in front of a chalkboard which reads "women are powerful and dangerous".

Marsha P. Johnson (1945–1992)

An American gay rights activist and champion of drag queen culture in New York City, she was a key figure in the Stonewall uprising of 1969 and an AIDS activist with ACT UP. When her body was found in the Hudson River, her death, which was ruled a suicide, was believed by many to be foul play. The case was re-opened in 2012.

Ana Mendieta (1948–1985)

A Cuban-American performance artist whose works were heavily influenced by the female form and the natural world. She produced over 200 works of art during her lifetime. She died after falling from her 34th-floor apartment. Her husband, Carl Andre, who allegedly pushed her, was acquitted of the crime.

Shireen Abu Akleh (1971–2022)

An award-winning Palestinian-American journalist, she worked as a reporter for Al-Jazeera for over twenty years. She was shot and killed by Israeli forces while covering the raid of a refugee camp in the West Bank.

Cay Bluestocking is an American-born writer and public historian based in the United Kingdom. She received the Rising Star award from the Nature of Words at the age of 15. Her previous publications include various short stories and poems for Creative Communications, It's All Write, Outlet and RiPPLE. In 2020, she was included in the largest anthology of poets in the world for *Poets for Peace* and won the ArtCabbage 2024 award in the category of Literature. She works as a supporting writer and actress for the Other Mysteries Theatre Company and as a representative for young artists and creatives through The Humanities Guild. Cay can be found on all social media platforms at @CayBluestocking where she makes informative and comedic content about history, art, culture, and museums.

Printed in Great Britain
by Amazon

28642e62-28f3-4111-adfb-3109c2583348R01